LE GETTE'S
CHOLESTEROL ENCYCLOPEDIA

BERNARD · LE · GETTE

WARNER BOOKS

A Warner Communications Company

Warner Books, Inc.
666 Fifth Avenue
New York, N.Y. 10103

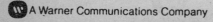 A Warner Communications Company

Printed in the United States of America

First Printing: February, 1989
10 9 8 7 6 5 4 3 2 1

Heart attacks . . . strokes . . . aneurysms . . .
We all know that a diet high in cholesterol can lead to these
and other life-threatening vascular diseases. But do you
know which foods are the real cholesterol culprits? Which
unexpected foods you can enjoy if the *quantity* is right? And
which healthful foods actually work to *reduce* your cholesterol level? It's all here in
LE GETTE'S CHOLESTEROL ENCYCLOPEDIA.
**Now, take the cholesterol quiz—
the answers may surprise you!
Can you choose the meals with the least cholesterol?**

BREAKFAST

Scrambled Eggs (medium) English Muffin with Apple Butter Orange Juice	Homemade Waffles with 1 tbsp. Butter Cocoa (with Whole Milk)

LUNCH

(At McDonald's) Cheeseburger French Fries Coke	*(At Long John Silver's)* Seafood Salad Coffee

DINNER

Broiled Beef Tenderloin (4 ounces/lean) Uncle Ben's Rice Green Salad with Italian Dressing Brown & Serve Roll with 1 tbsp. Whipped Butter Wine Banana Cream Pie (1 piece)	Broiled Liver (Beef/4 ounces) Minute Rice Green Salad with Roka Blue Cheese Dressing Croissant with 1 tbsp. Butter Milk (8-ounce glass) Frozen Yogurt Bar (Columbo/Vanilla)

PLEASE TURN THE PAGE FOR THE CORRECT ANSWERS.

ANSWERS: *Breakfast*: The waffle breakfast is a winner with only 140 milligrams of cholesterol; the scrambled eggs are packed with 247 milligrams. *Lunch*: Salads may be healthy, but this one contains 113 milligrams, 63 more than the cheeseburger and fries. *Dinner*: Believe it or not, the liver dinner delivers three times as much cholesterol as the tenderloin meal.

Don't let cholesterol sneak up on you . . .
    turn to LE GETTE'S CHOLESTEROL ENCYCLOPEDIA

Also by Bernard Le Gette

Le Gette's Calorie Encyclopedia

Le Gette's Guide to Fresh Food Shopping

Published by
WARNER BOOKS

Contents

Contents

Introduction

Most foods contain very little cholesterol. There are no complicated minefields to negotiate, as with calories, say, where foods that are apparently similar can differ wildly in their calorie counts. With cholesterol it's pretty simple. Even the most casual look at the Fingertip Guide (the last chapter in this book) will show how easy it is to eat the amount of cholesterol you want—always.

In addition, there are two rules of thumb to make it even easier. First, avoid eggs and animal organs (such as liver and brains). Second, remember that if it grows in the ground, it contains no cholesterol.

Now most people will find that giving up a daily egg and brain sandwich is not a serious hardship. But what about cheese and fried chicken? How do you stop eating things like that? Well, I don't think you have to, at least not to cut down your cholesterol intake. Most cheese, for instance, is not extraordinarily high in cholesterol. The problem most people have with cheese is the quantity. If you can keep it down to the snack it probably should be, and not make a meal of it, you can enjoy it and not take in so much cholesterol. With chicken or anything else that's fried, just make sure it's fried in vegetable oil or seed oil. Most people use olive or corn oil, but there are a zillion others: walnut, avocado, sunflower, safflower, and on and on. And they're all as delicious as butter, and certainly more so than lard.

That brings us, however, to another consideration. Lowering the cholesterol in your blood will lower your risk of heart attack. Actually there are three kinds of cholesterol. You want to lower two of them and raise the third, called HDL (high-density lipoproteins). Fortunately, most of the things that lower the two also raise the third, so we don't have to get into that here.

The real question is whether lowering your intake of cholesterol in food will lower the cholesterol in your blood. You would think it would, but not always. With some people it does, and with some people it doesn't. So what do you do? There are three things:

1) Lower your cholesterol intake anyway. In any method to lower your blood cholesterol, lowering your food cholesterol is the first requirement.

2) Eat less saturated fat. That's mostly animal fat, and palm and coconut oils. A good rule of thumb is that if it's hard at room temperature (animal fat, butter, lard, etc.), it's probably saturated fat. You also want to avoid peanut oil—it's not saturated, but it's an exception.

3) Eat more of the following:

polyunsaturated fat—that's the dominant fat in most vegetable oils and fish.

monounsaturated fat—olive oil and soybean oils are excellent sources. Both polyunsaturated and monounsaturated fats lower the first two kinds of cholesterol, and monounsaturated actually raises HDL.

fish—5%–40% of the fat in fish is Omega-3 fatty acids. This is perhaps the most unsaturated fat of all and is particularly beneficial in lowering unwanted cholesterol and another thing, called triglycerides, which you don't want either.

oat bran

dried beans, barley, and lentils

grapefruit

garlic

onions

yogurt

vitamin C, chromium, and magnesium

These things also have been shown to reduce unwanted cholesterol.

In addition, consistent aerobic exercise and keeping your weight down will help.

You don't have to go crazy with this stuff. Merely leaning in the direction I just suggested will help. How far you want to lean, and how much you want to learn about it is up to you.

In any case, the first ingredient in all this is simply to lower your cholesterol intake. Use the Fingertip Guide, throw in a little common sense, and you'll probably be healthier.

LE GETTE'S
CHOLESTEROL
ENCYCLOPEDIA

CHAPTER 1

Beverages

Alcohol
   Spirits, wines, liqueurs, brandies, beer, and ale   0
Cocktail Mixes   0
Soft Drinks   0
Coffee and Tea   0
Fruit and Vegetable Juices   0
Fruit-Flavored Drinks   0

CHAPTER 2

Dairy

BUTTER AND MARGARINE

Butter
  ½ cup (¼ lb)   **248**
  1 Tbsp   **31**
Butter, whipped
  ½ cup   **165**
  1 Tbsp   **20**
Butter buds   **0**
Margarine, 1 Tbsp
  vegetable fats   **0**
  ⅔ animal fats   **6**

CHEESE, 1 oz unless noted

American
Kraft	25
Land O Lakes	25
Laughing Cow	28
Sargento	27

Blue
Dorman's	21
Frigo	21
Kraft	30
Sargento	21

Brick	27
Brie	28
Camembert	21
Caraway	30
Cheddar	30
Cheddar (*Weight Watchers* shredded)	28
Cheshire	29

Colby
Dorman's	27
Kraft	30
Land O Lakes	25
Sargento	27

Cottage, 4 oz	23
Cottage, low fat, 4 oz	15

Cream Cheese	31
Edam	25
Farmer's	26
Feta	25
Fontina	33
Gorgonzola	21
Gouda	30
Gruyere	31
Havarti	
Casino	35
Sargento	21
Italian Blend	20
Jarlsberg	16
Limburger	26
Monterey Jack	
Kraft	30
Land O Lakes	20
Sargento	30
Mozzarella	
whole milk	25
part skim	15
Muenster	
Kraft	30
Land O Lakes	25
Sargento	27
Neufchatel	22
Parmesan, natural	19
Parmesan, grated	

Frigo	23
Kraft	30
Sargento	22
Universal	25
Port du Salut	35
Provolone	
Dorman's	20
Kraft	25
Land O Lakes	20
Sargento	20
Ricotta	
whole milk	15
part skim	10
low fat	5
Romano	30
Roquefort	26
Scamorze	15
String	15
Swiss	26
Taco	28
Tilsit	29

Cheese Food

American	
Dorman's	6
Harvest Moon	15

Kraft Singles	20
Kraft grated	10
American with Bacon	20
Cheddar	
Kraft Cracker Barrel	20
Land O Lakes	20
Light 'n Lively	15
Weight Watchers	8
Jalapeño	
Kraft	25
Land O Lakes	20
Pimiento	
Kraft	20
Salami	
Land O Lakes	20
Sharp	
Kraft	20
Swiss	
Kraft	25
Light 'n Lively	15
Velveeta	20

Cheese Spread

American	
Kraft	20
Land O Lakes	70

CREAM, 1 Tbsp

half and half	6
light	10
medium	17
heavy (whipping)	
whipped	10
unwhipped	20

Sour Cream   5

half and half	8
imitation	0

Non-Dairy Creamers, 1 Tsp   0

EGGS

Chicken
  raw, boiled, or poached
    medium   **235**
    large   **270**
    extra large   **300**
  raw, white only   **·0**
  fried or scrambled
    medium   **247**
    large   **282**
    extra large   **312**
Duck   **600**
Quail   **75**
Turkey   **725**

Egg Mixes, Commercial

Imitation
  Fleischmann's Egg Beaters   **0**
Omelets
  Home Recipe, 1 serving   **582**
Scrambled
  Jack in the Box, 1 serving   **260**

MILK, 8 oz

Buttermilk
   1% fat   10
   2% fat   20
   3.5% fat   38

Buttermilk	
1% fat	10
2% fat	20
3.5% fat	38
Condensed, 1 oz	6
Evaporated	
unsweetened	75
Carnation	62
Carnation, skim	2
Goat	26
Skim	10
Whole, 3.5% fat	33

Milk Beverages, 8 oz unless noted

Chocolate	
1% fat	5
2% fat	18
3.5% fat	30
Cocoa, with whole milk	34
Carnation 70 Calorie Mix, with water	2
Swiss Miss, with water	0
Egg Nog, with whole milk	150
Egg Nog, *Land O Lakes*	123
Malted, with whole milk	34
Horlicks Instant Chocolate	2

YOGURT

Columbo
   whole milk, 3.5 oz   9
   Nonfat Lite, 3.5 oz   0
Dannon
   whole milk, 8 oz   10
   whole milk Mini-Pack, 4.4 oz   5
   Extra Smooth, 6 oz   10
   Extra Smooth Mini-Pack, 4.4 oz   10

Frozen Yogurt, 1 bar

Columbo
   Sorbet Swirl   0
   Tofree   0
   Vanilla   7
Danny
   On-A-Stick   5
Sealtest   5
Yoplait   15

CHAPTER 3

Breads and Cereals

BREAD AND BISCUITS

Virtually all bread and biscuits contain between 0 and 5 milligrams of cholesterol per piece.

MUFFINS AND ROLLS

Muffins, 1 muffin

Blueberry
Hostess   15

Morton	
regular	9
Rounds	14
Bran	
Arnold	0
Duncan Hines (mix)	0
Corn	
Morton	14
English	0
Raisin	0
Roman Meal	0
Sourdough	0

Rolls, 1 roll

Hard Roll	1
Brown & Serve	0
Croissant	13
Dinner	2
Hamburger	0
Hoagie	0
Hot Dog	0
Hot Roll	
Pillsbury mix	9
Kaiser	
Wonder	5

CRACKERS, 1 piece

Bacon Nips	0
Butter	
Hi-Ho	0
Butter and Cheese	
Handi-Snacks	0
Cheddar Snack	
American Heritage	1
Cheetos	0
Cheez Balls	0
Cheez Curls	0
Cheez-It	0
Crispbread	
Wasa	0
Doritos	0
Garlic	
Manischewitz	0
Kavli	0
Matzos	
Manischewitz	
Egg	15
Egg 'N Onion	15
Miniatures	0
Passover unsalted	0
Tea Thins	0
Dietetic Thins	0

Wheat	0
Whole Wheat with Bran	0
Melba Toast	0
Onion	0
Oyster	
Sunshine	0
Parmesan	
American Heritage	0
Peanut Butter and Cheese	
Handi-Snack	0
Ritz	1
Roman Meal Wafers	1
Rye	0
Rye with Cheese	
Frito Lay	2
Saltines	0
Sesame	0
Soda	0
Tams	
Manischewitz	0
Town House	0
Triscuit	0
Wheat	0
Wheat with Cheese	
Frito Lay	1

OTHER BREAD PRODUCTS

Breadcrumbs   0
Croutons   0

FLOUR, all varieties   0

CEREAL

Cereal itself does not contain any cholesterol. Milk, cream, and butter of course do, and they are listed in Chapter 2: Dairy.

PANCAKES AND WAFFLES,
1 portion prepared as directed

Aunt Jemima	140
Hungry Jack	
Extra Lights	150
Mrs. Smith's	50
Roman Meal Waffles	
regular	4
Golden Delight	12
homemade pancakes	30
homemade waffles	75

CHAPTER 4

Beans, Pasta and Rice

BARLEY 0

BEANS
dried, canned, or frozen

**Black, Great Northern, Lima, Mung, Navy,
Pea, Pinto, Red Kidney, White, Blackeye Peas,
and Chick Peas** 0

PASTA

Except for egg noodles, pasta itself contains no cholesterol.

Egg Noodles, 1 cup

Muellers	65
Ronzoni	85

Macaroni and Cheese

frozen, 1 pkg

Morton

Casserole	24
Dinner	18
Family Size	80

mix, ¾ cup

Kraft

Dinner	5
Deluxe	20
Spirals	10
Velveeta Shells	25

RICE

Plain	0
Flavored	
Birds Eye	0
Rice-A-Roni	10
Mahatma	0
Minute Rice	10
Uncle Ben's	0
Bulgur	0
Kasha	0

CHAPTER 5

Soup

CANNED,
1 cup

Asparagus	5
Asparagus, cream of	22
Bean with bacon	3
Bean with franks	12
Bean with ham, chunky	22
Beef, chunky	14
Beef broth	0
Beef and mushroom	7
Beef noodle	5
Celery	15

Celery, cream of	32
Cheese	30
Chicken, chunky	30
Chicken and dumplings	34
Chicken gumbo	5
Chicken with mushroom	10
Chicken noodle	18
Chicken with rice	7
Chicken vegetable	17
Clam chowder, Manhattan	2
Clam chowder, New England	5
Clam chowder, New England with milk	22
Crab	10
Escarole	2
Gazpacho	0
Lentil	0
Lentil with ham	7
Minestrone	5
Mushroom	0
Mushroom, cream of	20
Onion	15
Pea	0
Pea, cream of	18
Pea with ham	7
Pepperpot	10
Potato	5
Potato, cream of	22
Shrimp	17

Stockpot	5
Tomato	0
Tomato, cream of	17
Tomato bisque, with milk	22
Tomato rice	2
Turkey	9
Turkey noodle	5
Turkey vegetable	2
Vegetable	0
Vegetable with beef	5

MIX,
1 cup

Asparagus, cream of	0
Bean with bacon	3
Beef bouillon	1
Beef noodle	2
Cauliflower	0
Celery, cream of	1
Chicken bouillon	1
Chicken noodle	3
Chicken with rice	3
Chicken with vegetable	3
Clam chowder, Manhattan	0
Clam chowder, New England	1
Consomme	0
Leek	2
Minestrone	3
Mushroom	1
Onion	0
Oxtail	3
Pea	3
Tomato	1
Tomato vegetable	1
Vegetable with beef	1

CHAPTER 6

Meat, Poultry and Seafood

MEAT, FRESH

Beef, choice-grade, retail cuts, 4 oz unless noted

Brisket
   whole   105
   flat half   101
   point half   108
Chuck, arm, roast or steak
   lean with fat   115
   lean only   112

Chuck, rib or blade
lean with fat	**120**
lean only	**117**

Club steak
lean with fat	**65**
lean only	**58**

Flank
lean with fat	**82**
lean only	**79**

Ground
with 21% fat	**107**
with 10% fat	**99**

Plate
lean with fat	**107**
lean only	**103**

Porterhouse
lean with fat	**94**
lean only	**91**

Rib roast
lean with fat	**98**
lean only	**93**

Round steak
lean with fat	**98**
lean only	**93**

Rump roast
lean with fat	**107**
lean only	**103**

Sirloin steak
  lean with fat   **107**
  lean only   **103**
T-bone steak
  lean with fat   **107**
  lean only   **103**
Tenderloin
  lean with fat   **98**
  lean only   **95**

Beef, prepared and specialty cuts

Brains, 4 oz	**2,350**
corned, cooked, 4 oz	**111**
dried, 4 oz	**72**
Hearts, 3.5 oz	**150**
Kidneys, 3.5 oz	**375**
Liver, 4 oz	**400**
Spleen, 4 oz	**390**
Suet, 1 oz	**18**
Sweetbreads (thymus), 4 oz	**250**
Tongue, 3.5 oz	
braised	**140**
smoked	**210**
tripe, 4 oz	**106**

Lamb, 4 oz

Leg
lean with fat	**102**
lean only	**95**

Loin chop
lean with fat	**109**
lean only	**105**

Rib
lean with fat	**105**
lean only	**98**

Shoulder
lean with fat	**111**
lean only	**109**

Heart	**171**
Kidney	**429**
Liver	**500**
Lamb's quarters	**0**
Sweetbreads (thymus)	**533**

Ham (see also Pork), 4 oz unless noted

Boiled, 1 slice	**15**

Fresh
lean with fat	**103**
lean only	**98**

Cured
   lean with fat   64
   lean only   59
Minced   60

Pork

Boston butt, shoulder
   lean with fat   107
   lean only   100
Loin chop
   lean with fat   110
   lean only   101
Loin roast
   lean with fat   116
   lean only   108
Picnic
   lean with fat   124
   lean only   116
Spareribs
   lean with fat   137

Pork, specialty cuts, 4 oz

Brains	**2,900**
Feet	
fresh, braised	**114**
pickled	**102**
Pancreas, braised	**355**
Spleen, 4 oz	**570**
Stomach	**215**

Veal, 4 oz

Chuck, lean with fat	**115**
Loin, lean with fat	**115**
Plate	**103**
Rib roast	**124**
Round	**115**

Veal, specialty cuts, 4 oz

Heart	**206**
Kidneys	**429**
Liver	**343**
Sweetbreads (thymus)	**533**

Cold Cuts, Sausages and other meats

Bologna, 1 slice	
Armour	15
Oscar Mayer	12
Bratwurst, 1 oz	
pork	17
pork and beef	19
Braunschweiger, 1 slice	50
Cervelat, 1 oz	19
Frankfurters, 1 frank	
Oscar Mayer	27
Armour	25
Frog's legs, meat only, 4 oz	57
Rabbit, 4 oz	74
Salami, 1 slice	15
Sausage	
Blood pudding	
4 oz	136
1 slice	30
Polish	80
Pork, 2 oz patty	40
Snails, steamed, 4 oz	150
Venison, raw, 4 oz	76

MEAT, COMMERCIALLY PACKAGED

Bacon, cooked, 1 slice	
thin	5
thick	10
Canadian	12
Bacon bits	
Oscar Mayer, 1 tsp	4
Corned beef, 1 oz	13
Beef, dried	18
Ham, lunch meat, 1 oz slice	16
smoked	20
Ham, canned, 1 oz	
Armour	17
Oscar Mayer	13
Ham patties, 1 patty	40
Ham salad, 1 oz	10
Ham steak, 1 oz	13
Ham and cheese loaf, 1 oz slice	16
Ham and cheese spread, 1 oz	10
Honey Loaf	
Oscar Mayer, 1 oz	12
Liver Cheese	
Oscar Mayer, 1 slice	75
Old-fashioned loaf, 1 slice	15
Olive loaf, 1 slice	10

Pastrami, 1 slice	26
Pâté, goose liver, 1 oz	43
Pepperoni, 1 oz	20
Pickle loaf, 1 slice	10
Vienna sausage, 1 sausage	8

Frozen Meat Entrees, 1 whole package, various sizes

Classic Lite	
Pepper steak	60
Steak Diane	90
Szechuan	70
Country Table	87
Dinner Classics	
Burgundy	95
Short ribs	95
Sirloin tips	100
Steak teriyaki	95
Stroganoff	90
Morton	
Dinner	66
Entree	35
Stouffer's Lean Cuisine Oriental	35

6

Meat Substitutes

Loma Linda
    meatless hotdog   0
Morningstar Farms
    Breakfast Links   0
    Breakfast Patties   0
    Breakfast Strips   0
Oscar Mayer Breakfast Strips, 1 strip   13
Sizzlean, 1 strip   5
Worthington
    Bolono   0
    Veg Skallops   0
    Vegetarian Burger   0
    Wham   0

POULTRY, FRESH

Chicken

Broiled or fried, 4 oz	**99**
Stewed, 4 oz	88
Gizzard, 1 oz	55
Heart	
1 heart	7
4 oz	275
Liver, 4 oz	715

Duck, roasted, 4 oz   96

Goose

roasted, 4 oz	106
liver, raw, 4 oz	484

Guinea hen, roasted, 4 oz   72

Pheasant, roasted, 4 oz   76

6

Quail, roasted, 4 oz   83

Squab (pigeon), roasted, 4 oz   105

Turkey, roasted, 4 oz

Dark meat	127
Light meat	98
Giblets	478
Gizzard	265
Heart	258
Liver	715

6

POULTRY, COMMERCIALLY CANNED, FROZEN, OR PACKAGED:

1 package unless noted

Chicken

Canned
Chun King Divider Pak	13
Chun King Stir-Fry	44

Frozen

Beatrice
Cordon Bleu	85
Parmigiana	50
Romanoff	55
Royale	50

Chun King
Chow Mein Boil-in-Bag	28
Oriental	26
Sweet and Sour	26

Classic Lite
breast, medallions in Marsala	85
breast, roast	85
Burgundy	70
Chow Mein	60
Oriental	65
Sweet and Sour	70

Country Table	**98**
Dinner Classics	
Fricassee	**75**
Sweet and Sour	**65**
Teriyaki	**70**
Lean Cuisine	
A La Orange	**45**
And Vegetables	**40**
Chow Mein	**60**
Glazed	**55**
Morton	
Boneless	**48**
Fried	**85**
Sliced	**98**
Pie	**36**

Turkey

Frozen dinners

Classic Lite	**70**
Country Table	**45**
Lean Cuisine	**70**
Morton	
Dinner	**66**
Entree	**27**
Pie	**40**

SEAFOOD, FRESH,
raw, meat only, 4 oz unless noted

Abalone	96
Bass, black, sea	46
Bass, fresh	78
Butterfish	74
Catfish	85
Caviar, sturgeon, 1 tbsp	48
Clams, 1 medium	38
Cod	94
Conch	160
Crab, deviled, 1 cup	250
Crab, Imperial, 1 cup	310
Crayfish	155
Croaker	69
Cusk	46
Eel	80
Eulachon, see Smelt	
Finnan Haddie	87
Flounder	57
Grouper	42
Haddock	65
Herring	92
Lake Trout	66
Ling Cod	59

Lobster	105
Mackerel	80
Mullet	56
Mussels	32
Ocean Perch	48
Octopus	54
Oysters	62
Perch	100
Pike	
Northern	45
Walleye	99
Pollack	81
Pompano	57
Rockfish	40
Roe, 1 oz	102
Sablefish	56
Salmon	
Atlantic	40
Chinook	75
Scallops	37
Sea Bass	46
Shrimp	170
Smelt	82
Snapper	42
Sole	57
Squid	264
Sucker, carp	46
Swordfish	44

Trout, Rainbow	65
Trout, Brook	63
Tuna	43
Whitefish	68

SEAFOOD, FROZEN DINNERS
1 package unless noted

Cod almondine, *Dinner Classics*	75
Fish Fillet, *Lean Cuisine*	
Divan	85
Florentine	100
Fish Dinner, *Morton*	74
Fish Sticks, 4 oz	127
Newburg, *Dinner Classics*	65
Shrimp Dinner, *Classic Lite*	110

SEAFOOD, CANNED

Crabmeat, 1 cup	136
Herring, 3 oz	75
Oysters, 1 cup	105
Salmon, 1 cup	
pink	130
red	80
Shrimp, 1 cup	160
Tuna, 2 oz	30

CHAPTER 7

Fruit and Vegetables

Fruits and vegetables by themselves,
whether fresh, frozen, or canned,
contain no cholesterol.

CHAPTER 8

Condiments, Dips, Dressings, Oils and Sauces

CONDIMENTS,
1 Tbsp, unless noted

Catsup	0
Celery flakes	0
Coriander	0
Curry powder	0
Garlic powder	0
Horseradish	0
Horseradish Sauce	
Sauceworks	5
Hot sauce	0
Mustard	0

Mustard Sauce
  Sauceworks 5
Onion salt 0
Parsley flakes 0
Pepper 0
Salt 0
Sandwich spread
  Hellmann's 5
  Kraft 5
  Oscar Mayer, 1 oz 10
Vinegar 0

DIPS, 1 oz

Avocado, guacamole	0
Bacon and horseradish	0
Blue cheese	10
Buttermilk	
Kraft Premium	20
Land O Lakes	7
Clam	
Kraft	10
Kraft Premium	20
Cucumber	
Kraft Premium	10
Dill	7
French Onion	
Kraft	0
Kraft Premium	10
Land O Lakes	7
Garlic	0
Jalapeño	
Kraft	0
Kraft Premium	15
Nacho Cheese	10
Onion and Garlic	4

SALAD DRESSINGS,
1 Tbsp unless noted

Bacon and buttermilk	0
Bacon and tomato	0
Bacon, creamy	0
Blue cheese	
Kraft	0
Roka	5
Wish-Bone	0
Blue cheese and bacon	0
Buttermilk	0
Caesar	
Bernstein Extra Rich	5
Kraft	0
Wish-Bone	0
Coleslaw	10
Cucumber	0
Cheddar and Bacon	0
French	0
Garlic	0
Italian	0
Mayonnaise	
Kraft	5
Hellmann's	5
Hellmann's Light	10

Weight Watchers	5
Oil and vinegar	0
Onion and chive	0
Roquefort	10
Russian	
Kraft	0
Weight Watchers	5
Wish-Bone	0
Sesame seed	0
Sour cream and bacon	0
Tartar sauce	5
Thousand Island	
Kraft	5
Weight Watchers	5
Wish-Bone	10

OILS
**All grain, nut, seed, and vegetable oils
contain no cholesterol.**

SHORTENING

Lard, 1 cup   195

SAUCES AND SEASONINGS
1 cup unless noted

Barbecue	0
Bearnaise (with milk and butter)	189
Chili	0
Clam	160
Cocktail	0
Hollandaise, *Jiffy*, 1 tbsp	8
Soy	0
Spaghetti	0
Spaghetti with meat	4
Steak sauce, *A-1*	0

Sweet and sour	0
Tabasco	0
Tartar, 1 tbsp	5
Teriyaki	0
White	0
Worcestershire	1

GRAVIES
¼ cup unless noted

au jus	0
beef	2
brown	2
chicken	2
pork	2
turkey	2

CHAPTER 9
Desserts, Baked Goods, Toppings, Candy and Ice Cream

BAKING MISCELLANY

Baking Powder	0
Yeast	0
Baking Chocolate	
Hershey's, 1 oz	4
Coconut	0
Ginger	0
Peanut Butter	0

CAKES
1 piece, approx ⅛ of cake

Boston Cream
  Mrs. Smith's, frozen   20
Cheesecake, Jell-O   30
Cherry Cheese
  Sara Lee, frozen   68
Doughnut, Earth Grains
  Cinnamon Apple   25
  Devil's Food   20
  Old-Fashioned   20

CAKE MIXES

Aunt Jemima
   Easy Mix Coffee Cake, ⅛ cake   **12**
Duncan Hines, 1/12 cake
   Angel Food   **0**
   Chocolate   **70**
   Devil's Food   **67**
   Devil's Food Lite   **46**
   Golden Butter   **90**
   Lemon Supreme   **70**
   Marble Fudge   **70**
   Strawberry Supreme   **70**
   White   **70**
   Yellow   **70**
Jell-O
   Cheesecake, ⅛ cake   **28**

CAKES FOR SNACKS,
1 cake

Hostess
Cupcake	4
Doughnut	
cinnamon	6
chocolate covered	4
Krunch	4
Old-Fashioned	10
Powdered Sugar	7
Hoho	13
Snoball	2
Twinkie	21
Little Debbie Snak Cake	0
Morton doughnuts, frozen	
Bavarian Cream	11
Boston Cream	11
Chocolate	10
Glazed	10
Jelly	11

COOKIES,
1 piece

Animal Crackers	0
Butter Flavor	0
Chocolate	0
Chocolate Chip	0
Custard	5
Fig Bar	
Sunshine	0
Fortune Cookie	0
Ginger Snaps	0
Graham	0
Lemon	0
Macaroon	0
Oatmeal	0
Peanut Butter	0
Sugar Wafers	0
Vanilla wafers	
Sunshine	1

PIES

Mrs. Smith's, 1 piece, approx ⅛ pie

Apple	**10**
Apple Natural Juice	**5**
Apple Old-Fashioned	**10**
Apple Streusel	**5**
Banana Cream	**5**
Blueberry	**10**
Boston Cream	**20**
Cherry	**5**
Chocolate Cream	**5**
Coconut Cream	**5**
Coconut Custard	**50**
Custard	**65**
Lemon Cream	**5**
Lemon Meringue	**35**
Peach	**10**
Pecan	**30**
Pumpkin Custard	**30**
Hostess **pies for snacks, 1 pie**	**18**

PUDDING, ½ cup

D-Zerta
chocolate	3
vanilla	2

Jell-O
banana	16
butter pecan	15
butter scotch	15
chocolate	17
coconut cream	15
golden egg custard	80
French vanilla	15
lemon	15
pineapple cream	15
pistachio	15
rice	15
tapioca	15
vanilla	15

Royal   14

CANDY,
1 piece

Baby Ruth	0
Butterfinger	0
Butterscotch Chips	0
Caramel	0
Crunch	
Nestle	5
Kisses	
Hershey's, 10 pieces	12
Milk Chocolate	25
Jelly Beans	0
Licorice	0
Lollipop	0
Marshmallow	0
Mint	0
Mr. Goodbar	5
Peanut Butter	
Reese's	2
Peanut Brittle	0
Peppermint	0
Raisins, chocolate-covered	1
Tootsie Roll	0
Gum	0

ICE CREAM, FROZEN CUSTARD AND ICE MILK, 1 cup

Ice Cream
  10% fat   40
  16% fat   84
Frozen Custard
  10% fat   97
Ice Milk
  hardened   26
  soft   35
Non-Dairy Ice Cream   0
Sherbet
  Dole   0
  Land O Lakes   10
  Shamitoff's   0
Sorbet   0

9

Nuts and seeds contain no cholesterol.

Dessert toppings, except for real cream, contain no cholesterol.

Jelly and gelatin contain no cholesterol.

Sugar, syrups, sweeteners, and honey contain no cholesterol.

SANDWICH SPREADS

Apple Butter	0
Hellmann's, 1 tbsp	5
Kraft, 1 tbsp	5
Oscar Mayer, 1 oz	10
Peanut Butter	0

CHAPTER 10

Fast Foods

1 serving

Arby's

Bac'n Cheddar Deluxe	78
Beef'n Cheddar Sandwich	70
Chicken Breast	57
Chicken Salad	12
Chicken Salad Sandwich	30
Club Sandwich	100
Chocolate Shake	32
French Fries	6
Ham 'n Cheese	60
Roast Beef Sandwich	45
Roast Beef Deluxe	59
Roast Beef Super	85

Turkey Sandwich	70
Vanilla Shake	30

Burger King

Apple Pie	4
Bacon Double Cheeseburger	104
Breakfast Croissanwich	
bacon, egg, cheese	249
ham, egg, cheese	262
sausage, egg, cheese	293
Cheeseburger	48
double	77
Cherry Pie	6
Chicken Sandwich	82
Chicken Tenders	47
Fish Filet	43
French Fries	14
French Toast	
with bacon	73
with sausage	115
Ham and Cheese	70
Hamburger	37
Onion Rings	0
Pecan Pie	4
Salad	0
with blue cheese	22
with Thousand Island	17

Scrambled Egg	370
with bacon	378
with sausage	420
Whaler	84
with cheese	95
Whopper	94
with cheese	117
Junior	41
Junior with cheese	52

Dairy Queen

Banana Split	30
Buster Bar	10
Cone	
small	10
regular	15
large	25
Dilly Bar	10
Double Delight	10
Float	20
Freeze	30
Hot Fudge Brownie Delight	20
Malt or shake	
small	35
regular	50
large	70
Mr. Misty	0
Parfait	30

Strawberry Shortcake	25
Sundae	
small	10
regular	20
large	30

Hardee's

Apple Turnover	5
Bacon Cheeseburger	60
Biscuit, Bacon and Egg	305
Biscuit, Cinnamon and Raisin	0
Biscuit, Egg	160
Biscuit, Gravy	21
Biscuit, Ham and Egg	293
Biscuit, Sausage	29
Biscuit, Sausage and Egg	293
Biscuit, Steak	34
Biscuit, Steak and Egg	298
Biscuit, Cured Ham	17
Big Cookie	9
Big Country Breakfast	
bacon	350
ham	369
sausage	442
Big Deluxe	50
Big Roast Beef	86
Cheeseburger	28
¼ pound	77

Fisherman's Fillet	80
French Fries	4
Hamburger	22
Hash Rounds	10
Hot Ham 'n Cheese	59
Mushroom 'n Swiss	86
Turkey Club	45

Jack In The Box

Bacon, 2 slices	10
Breakfast Jack	203
Canadian Crescent	226
Cheese Nachos	37
Cheeseburger	42
Cheeseburger Supreme	70
Chicken Supreme	60
Club Pita	43
French Fries	8
Ham and Swiss Burger	117
Jumbo Jack	64
with cheese	110
Moby Jack	47
Mushroom Burger	87
Pasta Seafood Salad	48
Taco	
regular	21
super	37
salad	102

Kentucky Fried Chicken

Original
breast, center   93
breast, side   96
drumstick   81
thigh   122
wing   67

Extra Crispy
breast, center   93
breast, side   66
thigh   121
wing   63

Nuggets   12
Nugget Sauce   1

Side Dishes
Baked Beans   1
Buttermilk Biscuit   1
Chicken Gravy   2
Cole Slaw   4
Corn on the Cob   1
Fries   2
Mashed Potatoes   1
Potato Salad   11

Long John Silver's

Fried Fish   31
Fried Shrimp   17
Fried Shrimp Dinner   127

Clam Chowder	17
Clam Dinner	27
Cole Slaw	12
Fish and Chicken	56
Fish and More	88
Fish Sandwich Platter	74
Hush Puppies	1
Kitchen Breaded Fish	25
Ocean Chef Salad	64
Oyster Dinner	75
3 Piece Fish Dinner	119
4 Piece Chicken Planks Dinner	25
6 Piece Chicken Nuggets Dinner	25
Scallop Dinner	37
Seafood Platter	95
Seafood Salad	113

McDonald's

Big Mac	83
Biscuit with	
Bacon, Egg and Cheese	263
Biscuit Spread	9
Sausage	48
Sausage and Egg	285
Cheeseburger	41
Chicken McNuggets	73
English Muffin with Butter	15
Filet O Fish	45

Roy Rogers

Chicken Thigh	85
and Leg	125
Chicken Wing	47
Egg and Biscuit Platter	284
with Bacon	294
with Ham	304
with Sausage	325
French Fries	42
Hamburger	73
Macaroni Salad	5
Pancake Platter	53
with Bacon	63
with Ham	73
with Sausage	93
Roast Beef Sandwich	55
with Cheese	73
RR Bar Burger	115

Wendy's

Bacon Cheeseburger	65
Breakfast Sandwich	200
Chicken Fried Steak	95
Chicken Sandwich	59
Chili	30
Double Hamburger	125
Fish Fillet	45
French Fries	15
French Toast	115

Home Fries	20
Kid's Meal Hamburger	20
Omelet, Ham and Cheese	450
and Mushroom	355
and Onion and Green Pepper	525
Taco Salad	40

CHAPTER 11
Fingertip Low Cholesterol Guide

FOOD WITH
NO CHOLESTEROL

Beverages

Alcohol
 Spirits, wines, liqueurs, brandies, beer, and ale
Cocktail mixes
Soft drinks
Coffee and tea
Fruit and vegetable juices
Fruit-flavored drinks

Dairy

Butter buds
Margarine, vegetable fats only
Sour cream, imitation
Non-dairy creamers
Egg white
Imitation egg
Cocoa, *Swiss Miss*, with water
Yogurt, *Columbo*, Nonfat Lite
Frozen yogurt, *Columbo*
   Sorbet Swirl
   Tofree

Bread and Biscuits

Bread
Muffins
   Bran
      Arnold
      Duncan Hines (mix)
   English
   Raisin
   Roman Meal
   Sourdough

Rolls
Brown and Serve
Hamburger
Hoagie
Hog dog
Crackers
Bacon Nips
Butter
Hi-Ho
Butter and cheese
Handi-snack
Cheetos
Cheese Balls
Cheese Curls
Cheez-It
Crispbread
Wasa
Doritos
Garlic
Manischewitz
Kavli
Matzos
Manischewitz
Miniatures
Passover unsalted
Tea Thins
Dietetic Thins
Wheat
Whole Wheat with Bran

Melba Toast
Onion
Oyster
  Sunshine
Parmesan
  American Heritage
Peanut Butter and cheese
  Handi-snack
Rye
Saltines
Sesame
Soda
Tams
  Manischewitz
Town House
Triscuit
Wheat

Other Bread Products

Breadcrumbs
Croutons
Flour, all varieties

CEREAL

All cereal

BEANS, PASTA AND RICE

Barley
Beans, dried, canned or frozen
  Black
  Great Northern
  Lima
  Mung
  Navy
  Pea
  Pinto
  Red Kidney
  White
  Blackeye Peas
  Chick Peas

PASTA

All pasta except egg noodles

RICE

All plain rice
Flavored
  Birds Eye
  Mahatma
  Uncle Ben's
Bulgur
Kasha

SOUP

Beef Broth
Gazpacho
Lentil
Mushroom
Pea
Tomato
Vegetable

Mix

Asparagus, cream of
Cauliflower
Clam Chowder, Manhattan
Consomme
Onion

MEAT

Meat, Fresh

Lamb's quarters

Meat Substitutes

***Loma Linda*, meatless hot dog**
Morningstar Farms
   Breakfast Links
   Breakfast Patties
   Breakfast Strips
Worthington
   Bolono
   Veg Skallops
   Vegetarian Burger
   Wham

FRUITS AND VEGETABLES

Acerolas (West Indian Cherries)
Amaranth
Apple
Apricot
Artichoke
Arugula
Asparagus
Avocado
Bamboo shoots
Banana
Bean sprouts
Beet greens
Beet
Blackberries
Blueberries
Broccoli
Brussels sprouts
Cabbage, Chinese
Cabbage, green
Cabbage, red
Cabbage, savoy
Cabbage, spoon (Bakchoy)
Cantaloupe
Carambola
Carissas (Natal plums)

11

Carrot
Casaba Melon
Cauliflower
Celeriac root
Celery
Chard, swiss
Chayote
Cherimoya
Cherries
Chervil
Chives
Coconut
Collards
Corn
Corn Salad
Crab apple
Cranberries
Cucumber
Currants
Dandelion greens
Dates
Dock (Sorrel)
Eggplant
Elderberries
Endive (Chicory)
Escarole
Fennel
Figs

Garlic
Gingerroot
Green (snap) beans
Gooseberries
Grapefruit
Grapes
Ground-cherries
Guava
Honeydew melon
Jack Fruit
Jerusalem artichoke
Jujubes (Chinese dates)
Kale
Kohlrabi
Kumqu
Leeks
Lemon
Lettuce
Lime
Loganberries
Loqats
Mango
Mushroom
Mustard green
Mustard spinach (Tendergreens)
Nectarines
New Zealand spinach
Okra

11

Onion
Orange
Papaw
Papaya
Parsley
Parsnips
Passion fruit
Peach
Pear
Peas
Pea pods (snow peas)
Pepper
Persimmon
Pigeon Peas
Pineapple
Pitanga (Surinam Cherries)
Plantains
Plum
Poke shoot (Pokeberry)
Pomegranate
Potato
Prickly pear
Prune
Pumpkin
Purslane leaves
Quince
Radish
Raisin

Raspberries
Rhubarb
Rose apple
Rutabaga
Sapodillas
Shallot
Soursop
Soybean curd (Tofu)
Spinach
Squash
Strawberries
Sugar apple (Sweetsop)
Swamp Cabbage
Sweet Potato
Tamarind
Tomato
Towel gourd
Turnip greens
Turniop
Vinespinach (Basella)
Water chestnut
Watercress
Watermelon
Wax (yellow) beans
Yam beans
Yam
Zucchini

CONDIMENTS

Catsup
Celery flakes
Coriander
Curry powder
Garlic powder
Horseradish
Hot sauce
Mustard
Onion salt
Parsley flakes
Pepper
Salt
Vinegar

Dips

Avocado, guacamole
Bacon and Horseradish (*Kraft*)
French Onion (*Kraft*)
Garlic
Jalapeño (*Kraft*)

Salad Dressings

Bacon and Buttermilk
Bacon and Tomato
Bacon, creamy
Blue cheese
  Kraft
  Wish-Bone
Bluccheese and Bacon
Buttermilk
Caesar
  Kraft
  Wish-Bone
Cucumber
Cheddar and Bacon
French
Garlic
Italian
Oil and Vinegar
Onion and Chive
Russian
  Kraft
  Wish-Bone
Sesame Seed
Sour cream and Bacon

11

Oil

All grain, seed, nut, and vegetable oils

Sauces and Seasonings

Barbecue
Chili
Cocktail
Soy
Spaghetti
Steak sauce, *A-1*
Sweet and Sour
Tabasco
Teriyaki
White

DESSERTS AND BAKED GOODS

Baking Miscellany

Baking powder
Yeast
Coconut
Ginger
Peanut butter

Cake

Angel Food
Little Debbie **Snak Cake**

Cookies, one piece

Animal Crackers
Butter flavor
Chocolate
Chocolate chip
Fig bar, *Sunshine*

Fortune cookie
Ginger snaps
Graham
Lemon
Macaroon
Oatmeal
Peanut butter
Sugar wafers

JELLIES, SYRUPS, TOPPINGS AND SPREADS

Dessert Toppings, except for real cream

Jelly

Gelatin

Sugar

Sweeteners

Syrup

Honey

Spreads

Apple Butter
Peanut Butter

CANDY, ICE CREAM AND NUTS

Candy, one piece

Baby Ruth
Butterfinger
Butterscotch chips
Caramel
Jelly Bean
Licorice
Lollipop
Marshmallow
Mint
Peanut Brittle
Peppermint
Tootsie Roll
Gum

Non-dairy Ice Cream

Sherbet

Dole
Shamitoff

Sorbet

NUTS AND SEEDS

All nuts and seeds

0–50 MG CHOLESTEROL

DAIRY

Butter and Margarine

Butter, 1 Tbsp	31
Butter, whipped, 1 Tbsp	20
Margarine, ⅔ animal fats, 1 Tbsp	6

Cheese, 1 oz

American	
Kraft	25
Land O Lakes	25
Laughing Cow	28
Sargento	27
Blue	
Dorman's	21
Frigo	21
Kraft	30
Sargento	21
Brick	27
Brie	28

Camembert	21
Caraway	30
Cheddar	30
Cheddar (*Weight Watchers* **shredded)**	28
Cheshire	29
Colby	
Dorman's	27
Kraft	30
Land O Lakes	25
Sargento	27
Cottage, 4 oz	23
Cottage, low-fat, 4 oz	15
Cream Cheese	31
Edam	25
Farmer's	26
Feta	25
Fontina	33
Gorgonzola	21
Gouda	30
Gruyere	31
Havarti	
Casino	35
Sargento	21
Italian Blend	20
Jarlsberg	16
Limburger	26
Monterey Jack	
Kraft	30

Land O Lakes	20
Sargento	30
Mozzarella	
Whole milk	25
Part skim	15
Muenster	
Kraft	30
Land O Lakes	25
Sargento	27
Neufchatel	22
Parmesan, natural	19
Parmesan, grated	
Frigo	23
Kraft	30
Sargento	22
Universal	25
Port du Salut	35
Provolone	
Dorman's	20
Kraft	25
Land O Lakes	20
Sargento	20
Ricotta	
Whole milk	15
Part skim	10
Low fat	5
Romano	30
Roquefort	26

Scamorze	15
String	15
Swiss	26
Taco	28
Tilsit	29

Cheese Food

American

Dorman's	6
Harvest Moon	15
Kraft Singles	20
Kraft grated	10
American with Bacon	20

Cheddar

Kraft Cracker Barrel	20
Land O Lakes	20
Light 'n Lively	15
Weight Watchers	8

Jalapeño

Kraft	25
Land O Lakes	20

Pimiento

Kraft	20

Salami

Land O Lakes	20

Sharp
  Kraft   20
Swiss
  Kraft   25
  Light 'n Lively   15
Velveeta   20

Cheese Spread

American
  Kraft   20
  Sargento   25
Cheddar
  Kraft   15
Gruyere   18
Limburger
  Mohawk Valley   20
Pimiento
  Kraft   15
  Squeeze-A-Snack   20
Sharp   20
Swiss   24
Velveeta   20

CREAM, 1 Tbsp

Half and half	6
Light	10
Medium	17
Heavy (whipping)	
Whipped	10
Unwhipped	20

Sour Cream 5

Half and half	8

MILK, 8 OZ

Buttermilk
  1% fat   10
  2% fat   20
  3.5% fat   38
Condensed, 1 oz   6
Evaporated
  Carnation skim   2
Goat   26
Skim   10
Whole, 3.5% fat   33

Milk Beverages

Chocolate
  1% fat   5
  2% fat   18
  3.5% fat   30
Cocoa with whole milk   34
  Carnation 70 calorie mix with water   2
Malted with whole milk   34
  Horlick's Instant chocolate   2

YOGURT

Columbo, whole milk, 3.5 oz	9
Dannon, whole milk, 8 oz.	10
Extra smooth, 6 oz	10

Frozen Yogurt, 1 bar

Columbo vanilla	7
Danny-On-a-Stick	5
Sealtest	5
Yoplait	15

MUFFINS AND ROLLS

Muffins, 1 piece

Blueberry
  Hostess   15
  Morton
    regular   9
    Rounds   14
Corn, *Morton*   14

Rolls, 1

Hard roll   1
Croissant   13
Dinner   2
Hot roll, *Pillsbury* **mix**   9
Kaiser, *Wonder*   5

Crackers, 1 piece

Cheddar snack, *American Heritage*	1
Matzo	
Manischewitz	
Egg	15
Egg 'n Onion	15
Ritz	1
Roman Meal Wafers	1
Rye with cheese, *Frito Lay*	2
Wheat with cheese, *Frito Lay*	1

PANCAKES AND WAFFLES,
1 portion

Mrs. Smith's	50
Roman Meal Waffles	
Regular	4
Golden Delight	12
Homemade pancakes	30

MACARONI AND CHEESE

Frozen, 1 pkg	
Morton	
casserole	24
dinner	18
Mix, ¾ cup	
Kraft	
dinner	5
deluxe	20
spirals	10
Velveeta Shells	25

RICE, flavored

Rice-A-Roni	10
Minute Rice	10

SOUP

Canned, 1 cup

Asparagus	5
Asparagus, cream of	22
Bean with bacon	3
Bean with franks	12
Bean with ham, chunky	22
Beef, chunky	14
Beef with mushroom	7
Beef noodle	5
Celery	15
Celery, cream of	32
Cheese	30
Chicken, chunky	30
Chicken with dumplings	34
Chicken gumbo	5
Chicken mushroom	10

Chicken noodle	18
Chicken with rice	7
Chicken vegetable	17
Clam chowder, Manhattan	2
Clam chowder, New England	5
Clam chowder, New England, with milk	22
Crab	10
Escarole	2
Lentil with ham	7
Minestrone	5
Mushroom, cream of	20
Onion	15
Pea, cream of	18
Pea with ham	7
Pepperpot	10
Potato	5
Potato, cream of	22
Shrimp	17
Stockpot	5
Tomato, cream of	17
Tomato bisque with milk	22
Tomato Rice	2
Turkey	9
Turkey noodle	5
Turkey vegetable	2
Vegetable beef	5

11

Mix, 1 cup

Bean with bacon	3
Beef bouillon	1
Beef noodle	2
Celery, cream of	1
Chicken bouillon	1
Chicken noodle	3
Chicken with rice	3
Chicken with vegetable	3
Clam chowder, New England	1
Leek	2
Minestrone	3
Mushroom	1
Oxtail	3
Pea	3
Tomato	1
Tomato vegetable	1
Vegetable with beef	1

MEAT

Cold Cuts

Blood pudding, 1 slice	**30**
Bologna, 1 slice	
Armour	**15**
Oscar Mayer	**12**
Bratwurst, 1 oz	
Pork	**17**
Pork and beef	**19**
Braunschweiger, 1 slice	**50**
Cervelat, 1 oz	**19**
Frankfurters, 1 frank	
Armour	**27**
Oscar Mayer	**25**
Ham, boiled, 1 slice	**15**
Salami, 1 slice	**15**
Sausage, pork, 2 oz patty	**40**

Meat, Commercially Packaged

Bacon, cooked, 1 slice	
thin	**5**
thick	**10**
Canadian	**12**

Bacon bits
  Oscar Mayer, 1 tsp   4
Corned beef, 1 oz   13
Beef, dried   18
Ham, lunch meat, 1 oz slice   16
  smoked   20
Ham, canned, 1 oz
  Armour   17
  Oscar Mayer   13
Ham patties, 1 patty   40
Ham salad, 1 oz   10
Ham steak, 1 oz   13
Ham and cheese loaf, 1 oz slice   16
Ham and cheese spread, 1 oz   10
Honey loaf
  Oscar Mayer, 1 oz   12
Old-fashioned loaf, 1 slice   15
Olive loaf, 1 slice   10
Pastrami, 1 slice   26
Pate, goose liver, 1 oz   43
Pepperoni, 1 oz   20
Pickle loaf, 1 slice   10
Vienna sausage, 1   8

Frozen Meat Entree, 1 package

Morton entree   35
Stouffer's Lean Cuisine Oriental   35

Meat Substitutes

Oscar Mayer breakfast strips, 1 strip   13
Sizzlean, 1 strip   5

POULTRY, COMMERCIALLY PACKAGED, 1 Package

Chicken

canned
  Chun King Divider Pak   13
  Chun King StirFry   44
Frozen
  Beatrice
    Parmigiana   50
    Royale   50
  Chun King
    Chow Mein Boil-in-Bag   28
    Oriental   26
    Sweet and Sour   26
  Lean Cuisine
    A La Orange   45
    And Vegetables   40

Turkey

SEAFOOD, FRESH
Raw, meat only, 4 oz unless noted

Bass, black, sea	46
Caviar, sturgeon, 1 Tbsp	48
Clam, 1	38
Cusk	46
Grouper	42
Mussels	32
Ocean Perch	48
Pike, Northern	45
Rockfish	40
Salmon, Atlantic	40
Scallops	37
Sea Bass	46
Snapper	42
Sucker, Carp	46
Swordfish	44
Tuna	43
Tuna, canned, 2 oz	30

CONDIMENTS, DIPS AND DRESSINGS

Condiments, 1 Tbsp unless noted

Horseradish sauce
  Sauceworks   5
Mustard Sauce
  Sauceworks   5
Sandwich Spread
  Hellmann's   5
  Kraft   5
  Oscar Mayer   10

Dips, 1 oz

Blue cheese   10
Buttermilk
  Kraft Premium   20
  Land O Lakes   7
Clam
  Kraft   10
  Kraft Premium   20

Cucumber
Kraft Premium   10
Dill   7
French Onion
Kraft Premium   10
Land O Lakes   7
Jalapeño
Kraft Premium   15
Nacho cheese   10
Onion and Garlic   4

Salad Dressings, 1 Tbsp

Blue cheese, Roka   5
Caesar, Bernstein Extra Rich   5
Coleslaw   10
Mayonnaise
Kraft   5
Hellmann's   5
Hellmann's Light   10
Weight Watchers   5
Roquefort   10
Russian
Weight Watchers   5
Tartar Sauce   5

Thousand Island
  Kraft   5
  Weight Watchers   5
  Wish-Bone   10

Sauces and Seasonings, 1 cup

Hollandaise
  Jiffy, 1 Tbsp   8
Spaghetti, with meat   4
Tartar, 1 Tbsp   5
Worcestershire   1

Gravy, ¼ cup   2

BAKING

Baking chocolate, *Hershey's*, 1 oz   4

CAKES,
1 piece, approximately ⅛ of cake

Boston cream
  Mrs. Smith's, frozen   20
Cheese cake
  Jell-O   30
Doughnuts, Earth Grains
  Cinnamon Apple   25
  Devil's Food   20
  Old-Fashioned   20

Cake Mixes

Aunt Jemima, Easy Mix, Coffee Cake   12
Duncan Hines Devil's Food Lite, ¹⁄₁₂   46
Jell-O cheese cake   28

Cakes for Snacks, 1 cake

Hostess
Cupcake 4
Doughnut
Cinnamon 6
Chocolate-covered 4
Krunch 4
Old-Fashioned 10
Powdered sugar 7
Hoho 13
Snowball 2
Twinkie 21
Morton doughnuts, frozen
Bavarian cream 11
Boston cream 11
Chocolate 10
Glazed 10
Jelly 11

COOKIES, 1 piece

Custard	5
Vanilla wafers	1

PIES

Mrs. Smith's, 1 piece, approximately ⅛ pie

Apple	10
Apple Natural Juice	5
Apple Old-Fashioned	10
Apple Streusel	5
Banana Cream	5
Blueberry	10
Boston Cream	20
Cherry	5
Chocolate cream	5
Coconut cream	5
Coconut Custard	50
Lemon cream	5
Lemon Meringue	35
Peach	10
Pecan	30
Pumpkin Custard	30
Hostess Cakes for Snacks, 1 cake	18

PUDDING, ½ cup

D-Zerta
Chocolate   3
Vanilla   2
Jell-O
Banana   16
Butter pecan   15
Butterscotch   15
Chocolate   17
Coconut cream   15
French vanilla   15
Lemon   15
Pineapple cream   15
Pistachio   15
Rice   15
Tapioca   15
Vanilla   15
Royal   14

11

SANDWICH SPREADS

Hellmann's, 1 Tbsp	5
Kraft, 1 Tbsp	5
Oscar Mayer, 1 oz	10

CANDY AND ICE CREAM

Candy, 1 piece

Crunch, *Nestle*	5
Kisses, *Hershey's*, 10 pieces	12
Milk chocolate	25
Mr. Goodbar	5
Peanut butter, *Reese's*	2
Raisins, chocolate-covered	1

Ice Cream, 10% fat 40

Ice Milk

hardened	26
soft	35

Sherbet

Land O Lakes	10

FAST FOODS

1 serving
Arby's

Chicken Salad	12
Chicken Salad Sandwich	30
Chocolate Shake	32
French Fries	6
Roast Beef sandwich	45
Vanilla shake	30

Burger King

Apple pie	4
Cheeseburger	48
Cherry pie	6
Chicken Tenders	47
Fish Filet	43
French Fries	14
Hamburger	37
Pecan Pie	4
Salad	
with Blue cheese	22
with Thousand Island	17
Whopper junior	41

Dairy Queen

Banana split	30
Buster Bar	10

Cone	
Small	10
Medium	15
Large	25
Dilly Bar	10
Double Delight	10
Float	20
Freeze	30
Hot Fudge Brownie Delight	20
Malt or Shake	
Small	35
Regular	50
Parfait	30
Strawberry Shortcake	25
Sundae	
Small	10
Regular	20
Large	30
Hardee's	
Apple Turnover	5
Biscuit, Gravy	21
Biscuit, Sausage	29
Biscuit, Steak	34
Biscuit, Cured Ham	17
Big Cookie	9
Big Deluxe	50
Cheeseburger	28

French Fries	4
Hamburger	22
Hash Rounds	10
Turkey Club	45

Jack In The Box

Bacon, 2 slices	10
Cheese Nachos	37
Cheeseburger	42
Club Pita	43
French Fries	8
Moby Jack	47
Pasta Seafood Salad	48
Taco	
Regular	21
Super	37

Kentucky Fried Chicken

Nuggets	12
Nugget Sauce	1
Baked Beans	1
Buttermilk Biscuit	1
Chicken gravy	2
Coleslaw	4
Corn on the Cob	1
French Fries	2
Mashed Potatoes	1
Potato Salad	11

Long John Silver's
Fried Fish	31
Fried Shrimp	17
Clam Chowder	17
Clam Dinner	27
Coleslaw	12
Hushpuppies	1
Kitchen Breaded Fish	25
4 Piece Chicken Planks Dinner	25
6 Piece Chicken Nuggets Dinner	25
Scallop Dinner	37

McDonald's
Biscuit	
with Biscuit spread	9
with sausage	48
Cheeseburger	41
English Muffin with butter	15
Filet 'o Fish	45
French Fries	9
Hamburger	29
McDonaldland Cookie	10

51–100

DAIRY

Cheese Spread, American
Land O Lakes   70
Milk, 8 oz
  Evaporated
    Unsweetened   75
    Carnation   62

EGGS

Quail   75

BREADS AND CEREALS

Homemade waffles   75

BEANS, PASTA, RICE

Egg Noodles, 1 cup
Muellers   65
Ronzoni   85
Macaroni and cheese, frozen, 1 package
Morton, family size   80

11

MEAT, fresh, 4 oz

Beef

Club steak
lean with fat	65
lean only	58

Dried 72

Flank
lean with fat	82
lean only	79

Ground, with 10% fat 99

Porterhouse
lean with fat	94
lean only	91

Rib roast
lean with fat	98
lean only	93

Round steak
lean with fat	98
lean only	93

Tenderloin
lean with fat	98
lean only	95

11

Lamb

Leg, lean only	95
Rib, lean only	98

Ham

Fresh, lean only	98
Cured	
lean only	64
lean with fat	59
Minced	60

Pork

Boston Butt, shoulder, lean only	100

Specialty Cuts

Frog's legs, meat only	57
Polish sausage	80
Rabbit	74
Venison	76

MEAT, COMMERCIALLY PACKAGED

Liver cheese, *(Oscar Mayer)* **1 slice**   75

Frozen

Classic Lite	
Pepper steak	60
Steak Diane	90
Szechuan	70
Country Table	87
Dinner Classics	
Burgundy	95
Short Ribs	95
Sirloin Tips	100
Steak Teriyaki	95
Stroganoff	90
Morton Dinner	66

POULTRY, fresh

Chicken
Broiled or fried, 4 oz   **99**
Stewed, 4 oz   **88**
Gizzard, 1 oz   **55**
Duck, roasted, 4 oz   **96**
Guinea hen, roasted, 4 oz   **72**
Pheasant, roasted, 4 oz   **76**
Quail, roasted, 4 oz   **83**
Turkey, roasted, 4 oz, light meat   **98**

POULTRY, COMMERCIALLY PACKAGED, 1 package

Frozen

Chicken
Beatrice
Cordon Bleu   **85**
Romanoff   **55**

Classic Lite
  Breast, Medallions in Marsala   85
  Breast, roast   85
  Burgundy   70
  Chow Mein   60
  Oriental   65
  Sweet and Sour   70
Country Table   98
Dinner Classics
  Fricassee   75
  Sweet and Sour   65
  Teriyaki   70
Lean Cuisine
  Chow Mein   60
  Glazed   55
Morton
  Fried   85
  Sliced   98
Turkey
  Classic Lite   70
  Lean Cuisine   70
  Morton Dinner   66

SEAFOOD, fresh, 4 oz

Abalone	96
Bass, fresh	78
Butterfish	74
Catfish	85
Cod	90
Croacker	69
Eel	80
Finnan Haddie	87
Flounder	57
Haddock	65
Herring	92
Lake Trout	66
Ling Cod	59
Mackerel	80
Mullet	56
Octopus	54
Oysters	62
Perch	100
Pike, Walleye	99
Pollack	81
Pompano	57
Sablefish	56
Salmon, Chinook	75
Smelt	82
Sole	57

Trout, Brook	63
Trout, Rainbow	65
Whitefish	68

Frozen, 1 package

Cod Almandine, *Dinner Classics*	75
Fish fillet, *Lean Cuisine*	
Divan	85
Florentine	100
Fish dinner, *Morton*	74
Newburg, *Dinner Classics*	65

Canned

Herring, 3 oz	75
Salmon, red, 1 cup	80

DESSERTS AND BAKED GOODS

Cakes, 1 piece

Cherry Cheese, *Sara Lee*, **frozen**   68

Cake Mix

Duncan Hines, ¹⁄₁₂ cake
Chocolate	70
Devil's Food	67
Golden Butter	90
Lemon Supreme	70
Marble Fudge	70
Strawberry Supreme	70
White	70
Yellow	70

Pies

Mrs. Smith's ⅛
  Custard   65

Pudding, ½ cup

Jell-O, Golden Egg Custard   80

ICE CREAM, 1 cup

Ice cream, 16% fat   84
Frozen Custard, 10% fat   97

FAST FOODS, 1 serving

Arby's
Bac'n Cheddar Deluxe	78
Beef 'n Cheddar Sandwich	70
Chicken breast	57
Club sandwich	100
Ham 'n Cheese	60
Roast Beef Deluxe	59
Roast Beef Super	85
Turkey Sandwich	70

Burger King
Double Cheeseburger	77
Chicken Sandwich	82
French Toast with bacon	73
Ham and Cheese	70
Whaler	84
with Cheese	95
Whopper	94
Whopper junior with cheese	52

Dairy Queen
Malt or shake, large	70

Hardee's
Bacon cheeseburger	60
Big roast beef	86

Cheeseburger, ¼ pound ... 77
Fisherman's Fillet ... 80
Hot Ham'n Cheese ... 59
Mushroom 'n Swiss ... 86

Jack in the Box

Cheeseburger Supreme ... 70
Chicken Supreme ... 60
Jumbo Jack ... 64
Mushroom Burger ... 87

Kentucky Fried Chicken

Original
  breast, center ... 93
  breast, side ... 96
  drumstick ... 81
  wing ... 67
Extra crispy
  breast, center ... 93
  breast, side ... 66
  wing ... 63

Long John Silver's

Fish and chicken ... 56
Fish and More ... 88
Fish Sandwich Platter ... 74
OceanChef Salad ... 64
Oyster dinner ... 75
Seafood platter ... 95

11

McDonald's

Big Mac	83
Chicken McNuggets	73
Mc D.L.T.	100
McMuffin, sausage	59
Quarter Pounder	81
Salad, Chicken Oriental	92

Roy Rogers

Cheeseburger	95
Chicken Nuggets	51
Chicken Thigh	85
Hamburger	73
Pancake platter	53
with bacon	63
with ham	73
with sausage	93
Roast beef sandwich	55
with cheese	73

Wendy's

Bacon cheeseburger	65
Chicken fried steak	95
Chicken sandwich	59

OVER 100

BUTTER

Butter, ½ cup (¼ pound)	**248**
Butter, whipped, ½ cup	**165**

EGGS, 1 egg

Chicken

raw, boiled or poached	
medium	235
large	270
extra large	300
fried or scrambled	
medium	247
large	282
extra large	312

Duck	600
Turkey	725

EGG MIXES, COMMERCIAL

Omelets, Home Recipe, 1 serving	582
Scrambled, *Jack in the Box*, 1 serving	260

MILK, 8 oz

Egg Nog, with whole milk	150
Egg Nog, *Land O Lakes*	123

PANCAKES AND WAFFLES,
1 portion

Aunt Jemima	140
Hungry Jack Extra Lights	150

MEAT, FRESH, 4 oz

Beef

Brisket
whole	105
flat half	101
point half	108

Chuck, arm, roast or steak
lean with fat	115
lean only	112

Chuck, rib or blade
lean with fat	120
lean only	117

Ground, with 21% fat 107

Plate
lean with fat	107
lean only	103

Rump roast
lean with fat	107
lean only	103

Sirloin
lean with fat	107
lean only	103

T-Bone
lean with fat	107
lean only	103

Beef, Specialty Cuts

Brains, 4 oz	2,350
Corned, cooked, 4 oz	111
Hearts, 3.5 oz	150
Kidneys, 3.5 oz	375
Liver, 4 oz	400
Spleen, 4 oz	390
Sweetbreads (Thymus), 4 oz	250
Tongue, 3.5 oz	
braised	140
smoked	210
Tripe, 4 oz	106

Lamb, 4 oz

Leg, lean with fat	102
Loin chop	
lean with fat	109
lean only	105
Rib, lean with fat	105
Shoulder	
lean with fat	111
lean only	109
Heart	171
Kidney	429
Liver	500
Sweetbreads (Thymus)	533

Ham

Boiled, 1 slice	**103**

Pork

Boston Butt, shoulder, lean with fat	**107**
Loin chop	
lean with fat	**110**
lean only	**101**
Loin Roast	
lean with fat	**116**
lean only	**108**
Picnic	
lean with fat	**124**
lean only	**116**
Spareribs, lean with fat	**137**

Pork, Specialty Cuts, 4 oz

Brains	**2,900**
Feet	
fresh, braised	**114**
pickled	**102**

Pancreas, braised	355
Spleen	570
Stomach	215

Veal, 4 oz

Chuck, lean with fat	115
Loin, lean with fat	115
Plate	103
Rib roast	124
Round	115

Veal, Specialty Cuts

Heart	206
Kidney	429
Liver	343
Sweetbreads (Thymus)	533

SAUSAGE AND OTHER

Blood Pudding, 4 oz   136
Snails, steamed, 4 oz   150

POULTRY, FRESH

Chicken

Hearts, 4 oz	**275**
Liver, 4 oz	**715**

Goose, 4 oz

Roasted	**106**
Liver, raw	**484**

Squab (pigeon), roasted, 4 oz   105

Turkey, roasted, 4 oz

Dark meat	**127**
Giblets	**478**
Gizzard	**265**
Heart	**258**
Liver	**715**

SEAFOOD, FRESH, 4 oz

Conch	160
Crab, 1 cup	
deviled	250
Imperial	310
Crayfish	155
Lobster	105
Roe, 1 oz	102
Shrimp	170
Squid	264

Frozen

Fish sticks, 4 oz	127
Shrimp dinner, *Classic Lite*	110

Canned, 1 cup

Crabmeat	136
Oysters	105
Salmon, pink	130
Shrimp	160

11

CONDIMENTS

Shortening

Lard, 1 cup   195

Seasonings, 1 cup

Bearnaise (with milk and butter)   189
Clam   160

FAST FOODS

Burger King
Bacon double cheeseburger   104
Breakfast Croissanwich
    Bacon, egg, cheese   249
    Ham, egg, cheese   262
    Sausage, egg, cheese   293
French toast with sausage   115
Scrambled egg   370
    with sausage   420
    with bacon   378
Whopper with cheese   117

Hardee's
Biscuit, Bacon and Egg   305
Biscuit, egg   160
Biscuit, ham and egg   293
Biscuit, sausage and egg   293
Biscuit, steak and egg   298
Big Country Breakfast
    bacon   350
    ham   369
    sausage   442

Jack in the Box
Breakfast Jack   203
Canadian Crescent   226

Ham and swiss burger	**117**
Jumbo Jack with cheese	**110**
Taco salad	**102**
Kentucky Fried Chicken	
Original, thigh	**122**
Extra crispy, thigh	**121**
Long John Silver's	
Fried shrimp dinner	**127**
3 piece Fish Dinner	**119**
Seafood salad	**113**
McDonald's	
Biscuit, with	
bacon, egg and cheese	**263**
sausage and egg	**285**
McMuffin	
egg	**259**
sausage and egg	**287**
Quarter Pounder, with cheese	**107**
Salad	
Chef	**125**
Shrimp	**187**
Garden	**110**
Scrambled eggs	**514**

Roy Rogers

Bacon cheeseburger	103
Breakfast Crescent Sandwich	148
with bacon	156
with ham	189
with sausage	168
Chicken breast	118
and wing	165
Chicken thigh and leg	125
Egg and biscuit platter	284
with bacon	294
with ham	304
with sausage	325
RR Bar burger	115

Wendy's

Breakfast sandwich	200
Double hamburger	125
French toast	115
Omelet, ham and cheese	450
and mushroom	355
and onion and green pepper	525